ENGLISH PLEAS

A Beginner's Course for Adults
Starter Book

Richard Harrison

LONGMAN

Longman Group Limtied,
Longman House, Burnt Mill, Harlow,
Essex CM20 2JE, England
and Associated companies throughout the world

First published 1995

Set in 12/15pt Avant Garde

Produced through Longman Malaysia, VVP

ISBN 0 582 24563 X

Printed in Hong Kong
NPC/01

Contents

To the Student

Welcome to *English Please!* a new English course for the Arab world. The course consists of three books: the Starter Book, Book 1 and Book 2.

Who is *English Please!* intended for?

It is intended for adults in the Arab World who are complete beginners, or who know just a little English.

Who is the Starter Book for?

The Starter Book is for those students who are not familiar with the English letters and numbers, or those students who would like more practice in forming the shapes.

What *is* the Starter Book?

The Starter Book is a preparation for Books 1 and 2 of the course. The main aims of the Starter are:

- to introduce and practise the numbers 0 to 10.

- to introduce and practise the letters of the alphabet (large and small letters).

The Starter also presents a number of useful everyday phrases for use in conversation - for example: "My name's... ", "What's the time?", "Where are you from?"

It also introduces some useful vocabulary. Many of the English words introduced are similar to words used in Arabic - for example: jacket, passport and video. You may be surprised. You already know more English words than you think!

Finally, the Starter Book also shows you how to use punctuation in English sentences and when to use capital letters (A, B, C,...) and when to use small letters (a, b, c,...).

عزيزي الطّالب

هذه السِّلسلة !English Please سِلسلة جديدة لأبْناء العالَم العربيّ ، وتتألَّف مِن ثلاثة كُتُب : الكِتاب التَّمهيديّ والكِتاب الأوَّل والكِتاب الثّاني .

لِمَن تَتوجَّه هذه السِّلسلة ؟

إنَّها للقُرّاء العرَب الرّاشدينَ المُبتدِئينَ بتَعلُّم اللُّغة الإنكليزيّة أو ذوي المَعرِفة اليَسيرة فيها .

لِمَن يَتوجَّه هذا الكِتاب التَّمهيديّ Starter Book ؟

يُفيد مِن هذا الكِتاب الطُّلاب غيرَ المُعتادينَ على الحُروف والأرقام باللُّغة الإنكليزيّة ، أو الّذينَ يَحتاجونَ المَزيد مِن المِران في هذا المَجال .

ما هو هذا الكِتاب ؟

إنَّه كِتاب تمهيديّ للوُصول إلى الكِتابينِ الأوَّل والثّاني مِن هذه السِّلسلة التَّعليميّة ، ويَرمي إلى :

– التَّعريف بالأرقام مِن صفر إلى ١٠ والتَّدريب عليها .

– التَّعريف بالحُروف الإنكليزيّة (الكَبيرة والصّغيرة) والتَّدريب عليها .

كما يَعرِض الكِتاب عدَدًا مِن العِبارات الشّائعة في لُغة التَّخاطُب اليَوْميّ ، مِثل : ...My name's (اسْمي ...) – the s'What time? (كَم السّاعَة ؟) – ?Where are you from (مِن أين أنْت ؟) .

ويُعطي الكِتاب كَذلك بعض المُفرَدات المُفيدة . ونُلاحِظ أنّ بعض الكَلِمات الإنكليزيّة نَستعمِلها ، بالصّيغة نَفْسِها ، وخُصوصًا في كَلامِنا العاميّ ، مِثل : Jacket و passport و video . فلِذلك لن تكون كُلّ الكَلِمات الإنكليزيّة غَريبة على مَسمَعِك !

بالإضافة إلى كُلّ ذلك ، يرشِدك الكِتاب إلى الاستِعمال الصّحيح لعَلامات التَّرقيم عند الكِتابة بالإنكليزيّة ، وإلى مَواضِع استِعمال الحُروف الكَبيرة (...A, B, C) والحُروف الصّغيرة (...a, b, c) .

How to use the Starter Book

كَيْفَ تَسْتَعْمِل هذا الكِتاب ؟

You can use the book in class with a teacher or working on your own at home. It is important to follow the instructions for forming a letter or a number.

يُمْكِن اعْتِماد الكِتاب في الصَّفّ مع وُجود مُدرِّس ، أو يُمكِنك الدَّرس به في البَيْت مِن دون مُدرِّس . ومِن الأهَمِيَّة بِمكان اتّباع التَّعْليمات للتوصُّل إلى الكِتابة الصَّحيحة للحُروف والأرْقام .

To help you draw the shapes correctly you are given sets of four lines to write on.

ولِمُساعَدتك على رَسْم الأشْكال بِالطَّريقة الصَّحيحة هُناك أربَعة أسْطُر للكِتابة .

The numbers and most of the letters rest on the solid line.

إنَّ كُلَّ الأرْقام ومُعْظَم الحُروف تكون قاعِدتها على السَّطر الثَّخين .

1   2   3   A   a

Arrows and dotted lines show you how to make the shapes of the numbers and letters.

وقد رُسِمَت السِّهام والخُطوط المُنَقَّطة لتَوْجيه حَرَكة اليَد عند الكِتابة .

A   a

Some small letters have "tails" which extend below the solid line.

وتَجدر المُلاحَظة أنَّ لِبَعْض الحُروف الصَّغيرة ذَيْلا يَنزل تحت السَّطر الثَّخين .

f   g   j   p   q   y

What will I be able to do by the end of the Starter Book?

غايَة هذا الكِتاب .

There are 26 capital letters (A to Z) and 26 small letters (a to z) as well as the numbers 0 to 9. By the end of the Starter Book you should be able to write them all clearly. You should also be able to join letters so as to write words, including your own name, the name of your city and the name of your country.

في اللُّغة الإنكليزيَّة ٢٦ حَرْفًا كَبيرًا (من A إلى Z) و ٢٦ حَرْفًا صَغيرًا (من a إلى z) بالإضافة إلى الأرْقام مِن صفر إلى ٩ ، وبالانْتِهاء مِن دِراسَة هذا الكِتاب سَتَتمكَّن مِن كِتابتها كُلّها بوضوح ، وكَذلك مِن وَصْل الحُروف لِكِتابة كَلِمات عَديدة مِن بَيْنِها اسْمك واسْم مَدينتك واسْم بَلَدك .

My name's Samira. I'm from Aswan in Egypt.

You will also be able to greet people in English and ask and answer a few simple questions. After that you should be ready to start Book 1 of *English Please!* Good luck!

وسَتَجِد أيْضًا أنَّك قادِر على التَّخاطُب باللُّغة الإنكليزيَّة في إلْقاء التَّحيَّة وطَرْح بعض الأسْئلة والإجابة عنها . وبعد كُلّ ذلك يُمكِنك الانْتِقال إلى الكِتاب الأوّل مِن سِلسلة *English Please!* . وفَّقَك الله وإلى المَزيد مِن التَّقدُّم .

Lesson 1

1   Left to right   مِن اليَسار إلى اليَمين

Left

Right

2

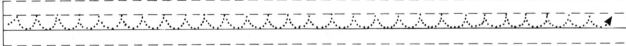

3

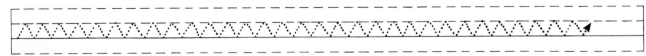

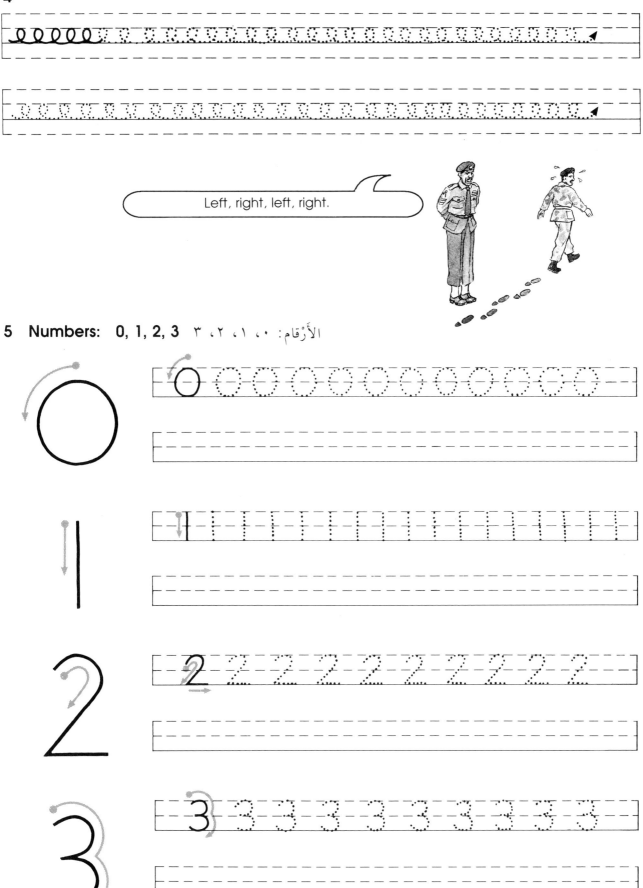

Left, right, left, right.

5 Numbers: 0, 1, 2, 3 الأَرْقام: ٠، ١، ٢، ٣

Lesson 2

1   Numbers: 4, 5, 6   الأرْقام: ٤، ٥، ٦

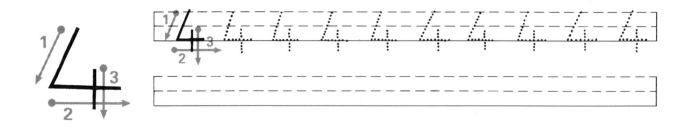

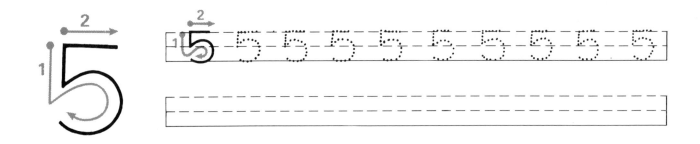

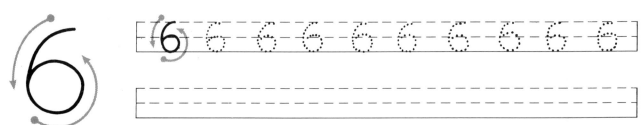

2   Match   ماﺋِلْ

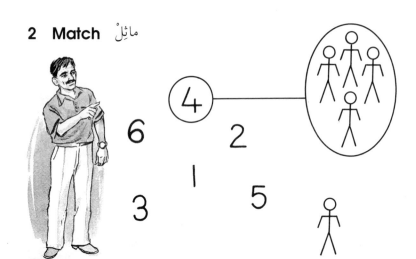

6   2

  1   5

3

4

3 Telephone numbers أرقام الهاتِف

4 Listen and write اِسْتَمِعْ واكْتُبْ

5 Write the licence number أُكْتُبْ رَقْم لَوْحَة السَّيَّارَة

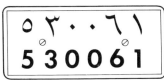

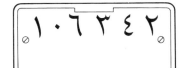

 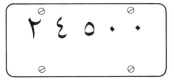

1   Numbers: 7, 8, 9   ٩ ، ٨، ٧ : الأَرْقام

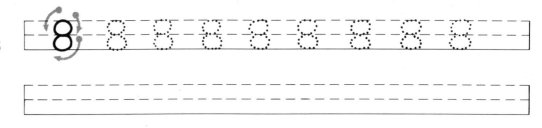

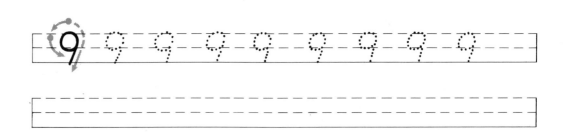

2   Match the numbers   ماثِلْ بينَ الأَرْقام

0	7	3	0	5	4	2	0	8	1	4	0	9	7	6	0
1	6	1	7	8	0	1	3	5	4	9	8	6	2	1	7
2	8	4	6	2	7	9	2	3	0	4	2	1	6	9	5
3	6	5	3	8	0	1	3	7	5	3	8	4	1	3	2
4	2	4	9	1	3	4	6	2	4	7	6	1	5	4	9
5	8	6	0	5	1	8	4	3	5	9	5	3	1	2	5
6	2	0	7	3	6	0	5	6	7	2	1	6	4	8	3
7	9	5	0	2	7	3	7	1	4	7	5	0	2	7	6
8	2	4	1	8	5	1	0	8	9	3	8	6	0	2	7
9	3	9	5	2	1	4	9	0	8	7	9	1	6	9	2

3 Write اُكْتُبْ

4 Listen and write اِسْتَمِعْ واكتُبْ

Telephone numbers

5 Write the licence number اُكْتُبْ رَقْم لَوْحَة السَّيَّارَة

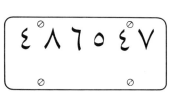

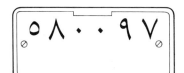

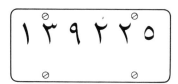

8

1 A B C

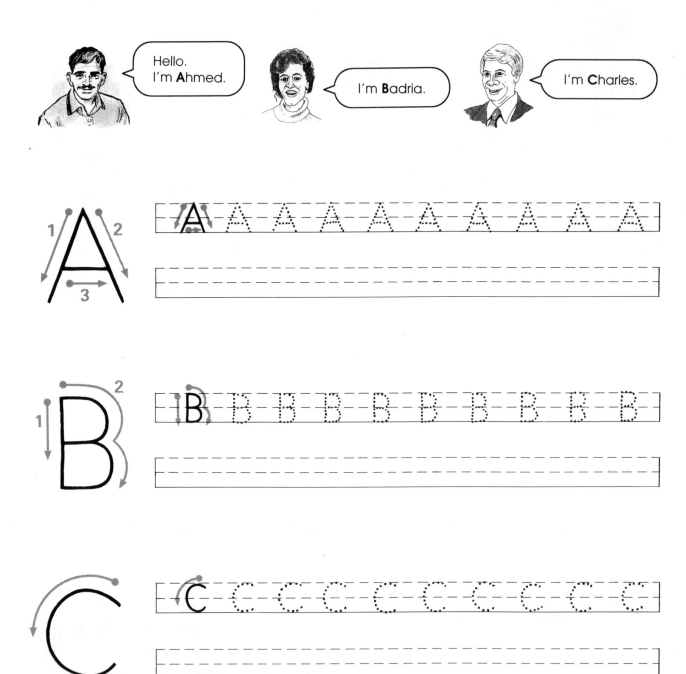

2 Match ماثِل

A	C	A̲	B	B	A	C	A	C	B	A	C	B	C	A	B	C
B	A	C̲	C	B	A	B	A	C	B	C	B	A	C	A	C	B
C	B	C	B	A	C	B	A	A	C	C	B	A	B	B	C	A

3 Listen and put an X اِسْتَمِعْ وضَعْ عَلامة ×

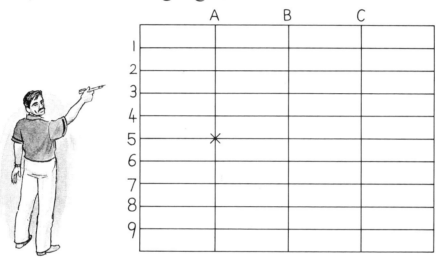

	A	B	C
1			
2			
3			
4			
5	×		
6			
7			
8			
9			

4 Listen and write اِسْتَمِعْ واكْتُبْ

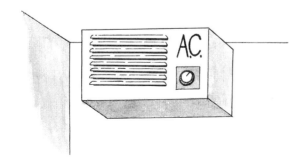

1 D E F

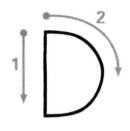 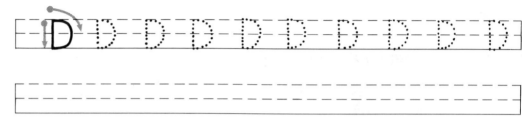

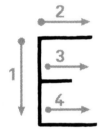 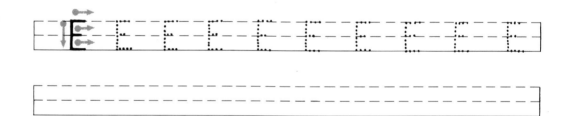

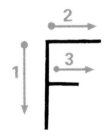 

2 Match مائِلْ

D	A	F	C	D	E	B	D	C	A	D	E	D	B	F	A	C
E		B	E	F	C	A	E	B	D	F	E	E	A	C	D	F	B
F		C	A	F	C	A	B	F	D	E	F	B	C	F	E	A	B

3 Match مائِلْ

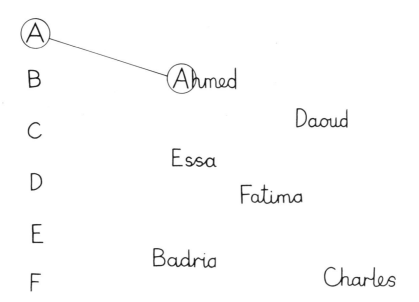

A ——————— (Ahmed)

B

C

Daoud

Essa

D

Fatima

E

Badria

F

Charles

4 Write اُكْتُبْ

A   C   D

5 Listen and write اِسْتَمِعْ واكْتُبْ

5 B.D.

12

Lesson 6

1 G H I

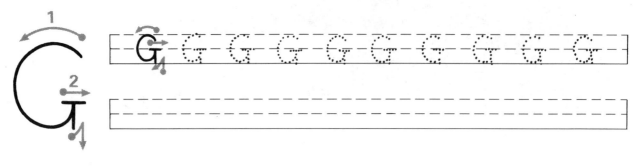

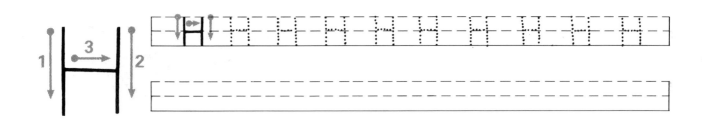

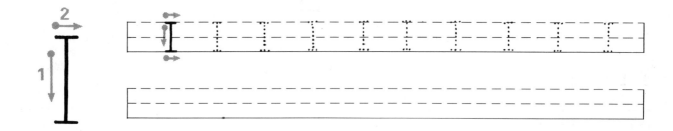

2   Match مَاثِلْ

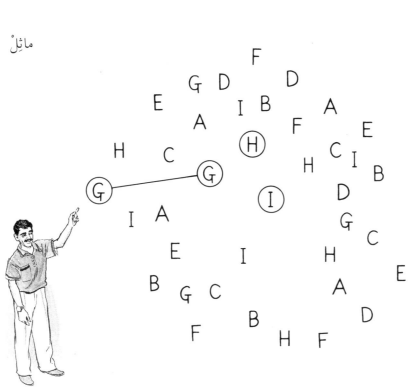

3   Listen and write اِسْتَمِعْ واكْتُبْ

4   Say قُلْ

1 J K L

JEDDAH 8K.

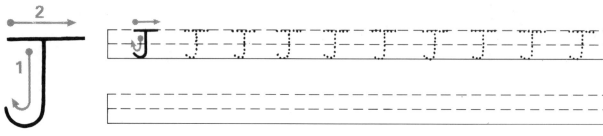

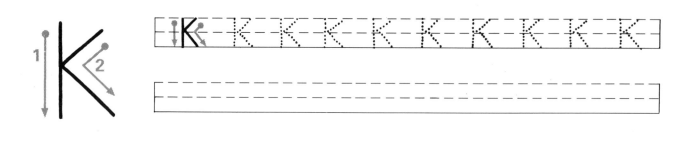

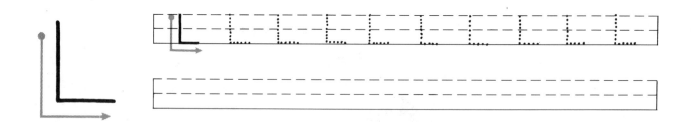

2 Match مائِلْ

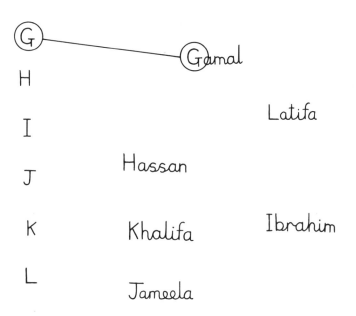

G ——— Gamal

H

                Latifa

I

      Hassan

J

K   Khalifa   Ibrahim

L

      Jameela

3 Write أُكْتُبْ

A   C   E F   H   J   L

4 Listen and write اِسْتَمِعْ واكْتُبْ

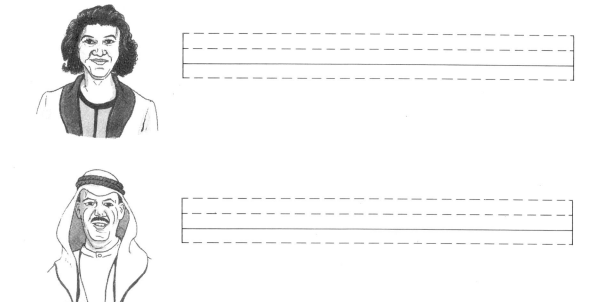

Lesson 8   Review   مُراجَعة

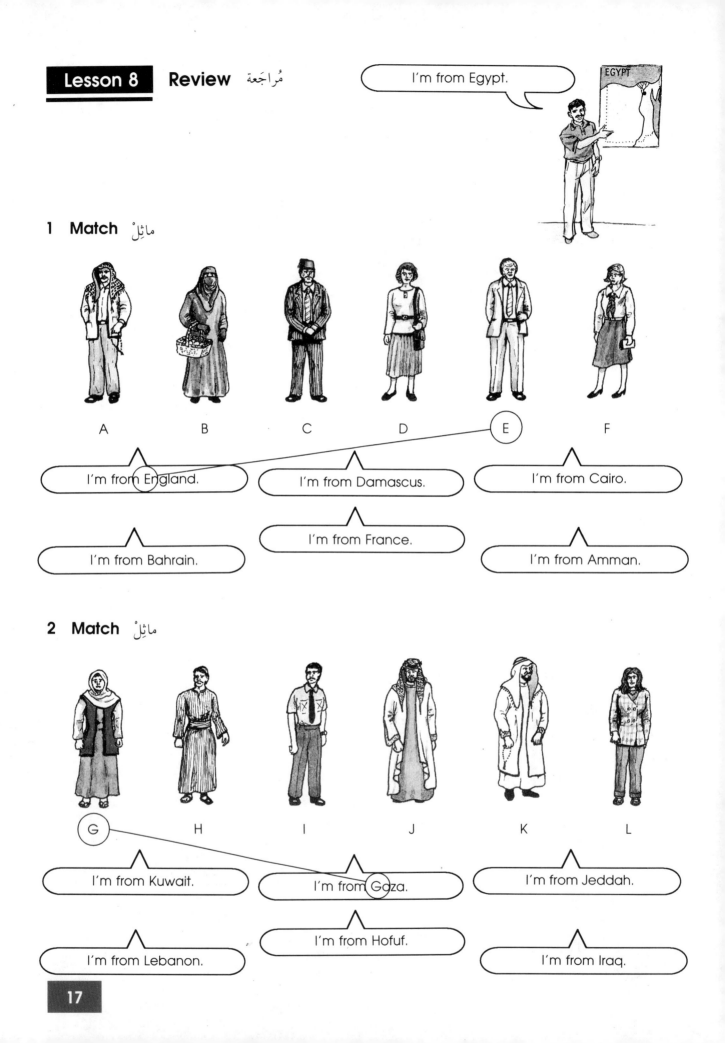

I'm from Egypt.

EGYPT

1   Match   ماثِلْ

A   B   C   D   E   F

I'm from England.

I'm from Damascus.

I'm from Cairo.

I'm from Bahrain.

I'm from France.

I'm from Amman.

2   Match   ماثِلْ

G   H   I   J   K   L

I'm from Kuwait.

I'm from Gaza.

I'm from Jeddah.

I'm from Lebanon.

I'm from Hofuf.

I'm from Iraq.

17

3 Match مائِل

A	B	K	F	<u>A</u>	G	I	H	A	L	E	A	B	H	K	F	A
B	E	A	J	B̲	I	D	B	C	E	G	B	I	F	D	B	G
C	F	G	L	C	I	G	C	K	H	B	D	C	G	B	C	K
D	B	D	E	I	A	D	F	B	D	C	J	G	L	D	E	C
E	F	I	J	E	H	B	L	K	E	I	J	E	L	F	B	E
F	B	A	K	H	F	D	E	F	B	G	D	L	F	A	E	F
G	K	C	B	G	A	D	B	G	J	L	E	C	G	A	G	D
H	I	A	H	L	K	H	J	E	A	D	K	E	H	H	I	B
I	E	B	I	A	C	I	J	L	C	I	D	E	L	K	J	I
J	L	J	A	I	J	H	A	I	J	C	B	E	J	L	B	H
K	A	E	K	F	H	J	K	C	A	K	E	H	A	K	L	J
L	F	L	I	D	L	E	C	L	A	I	J	K	B	E	J	L

4 Listen and write اِسْتَمِعْ واكْتُبْ

5 Listen and write اِسْتَمِعْ واكْتُبْ

	Flight Number
Damascus	_ _ _ _ _ _ _
Cairo	_ _ _ _ _ _ _
Jeddah	_ _ _ _ _ _ _
Kuwait	_ _ _ _ _ _ _
Bahrain	_ _ _ _ _ _ _

1 M N O

My name's Mary.

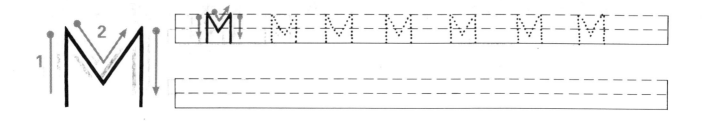

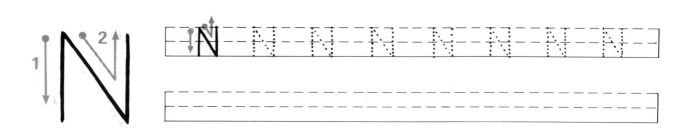

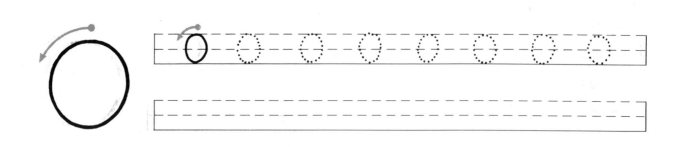

2 Match ماثِل

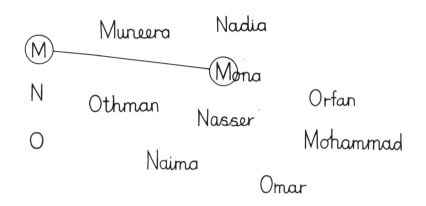

Muneera
Nadia
Ⓜ——————Ⓜona
N
Othman
Nasser
Orfan
O
Mohammad
Naima
Omar

3 Say قُلْ

A

Hello. My name's . . . .

B

Hello, ... My name's . . . .

4 Say قُلْ

A H J K
B C D E G
F L M N
I

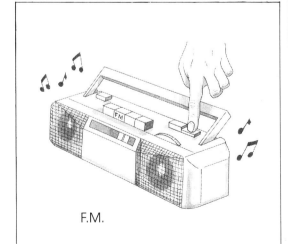

F.M.

Are you OK?

No!

1 P Q R

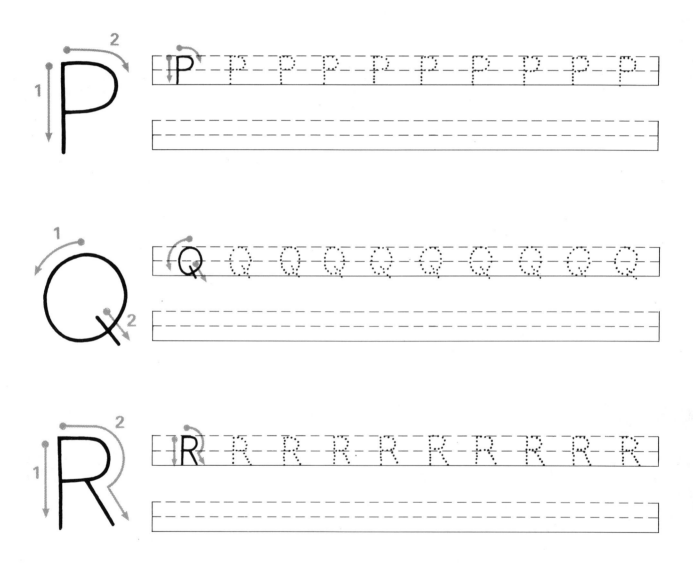

2 Match ماثِلْ

M	K	H	F	<u>M</u>	P	N	A	B	M	C	D	M	F	N	M	H
N	C	E	N	L	K	H	M	B	N	N	M	I	A	N	M	K
O	D	D	B	C	Q	P	O	C	D	B	Q	O	C	O	P	Q
P	F	L	R	P	K	F	R	P	J	B	D	P	B	M	P	R
Q	O	A	Q	P	C	G	Q	O	B	R	Q	G	O	Q	Q	H
R	K	J	M	R	P	F	K	R	J	A	R	P	O	F	K	R

3 Match ماثِلْ

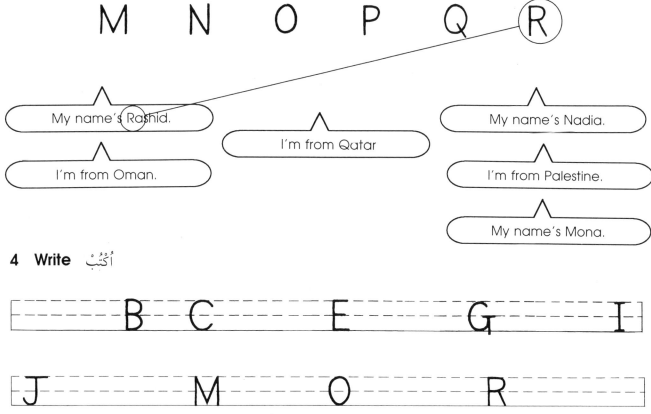

M N O P Q (R)

My name's Rashid.

I'm from Oman.

I'm from Qatar

My name's Nadia.

I'm from Palestine.

My name's Mona.

4 Write اُكْتُبْ

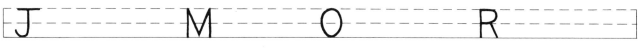

B C E G I

J M O R

5 Say قُلْ

P   B

M   N

P B

Listen and write اِسْتَمِعْ واكْتُبْ

1 ____ . ____ . ____ . C. ____ .

2 ____ A ____ ____ ____ A

1 S T U

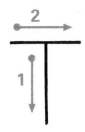
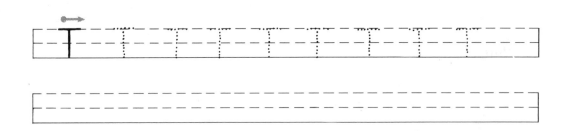

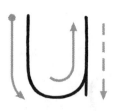
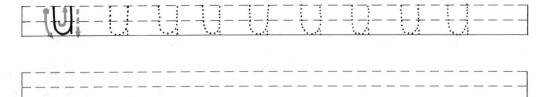

2 Match مائِلْ

S	B	P	S	E	C	D	E	S	R	Q	D	S	P	B	S	C
T	I	J	H	A	T	I	H	L	T	J	P	T	H	T	L	F
U	Q	C	U	J	D	B	U	A	L	G	Q	U	O	G	U	J

3 Match مائِلْ

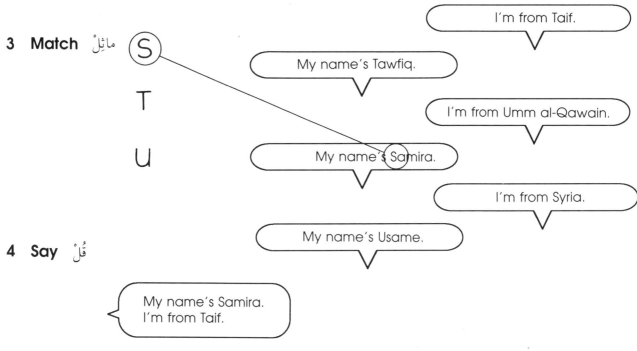

S

T

U

My name's Tawfiq.

I'm from Taif.

I'm from Umm al-Qawain.

My name's Samira.

I'm from Syria.

My name's Usame.

4 Say قُلْ

My name's Samira.
I'm from Taif.

My name's . . .
I'm from . . .

5 Listen and write اِسْتَمِعْ واكْتُبْ

U.A.E.

GO   STOP

Lesson 12

Welcome!

1 V W

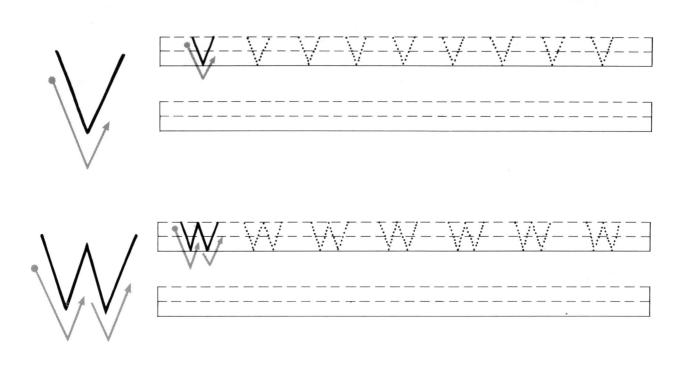

2 Match اُكْتُبْ

V   A   W   U   V   M   N   V   O   P   V   W   A   L   U   A   W   V

W   V   U   W   M   K   W   N   V   M   W   K   M   U   W   N   A   T

3 Listen and write اِسْتَمِعْ واكْتُبْ

4 Write اُكْتُبْ

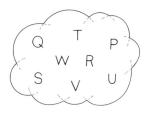

A B C D E F G H I J K L M N O

5 Write اُكْتُبْ

TV, BMW, VIP

_____

_____

_____

CAIRO AIRPORT

I'm Ahmed. Welcome to Cairo!

My name's Waleed.

Lesson 13

1 X Y Z

2 **Match** مائِل

X   Y   A   <u>X</u>   W   H   R   T   X   Y   V   X   W   B   X   Y   A
Y   V   W   Y   E   A   Y   K   V   S   A   Y   K   N   W   M   Y
Z   J   S   G   Z   S   T   E   Z   B   K   S   N   Z   V   Z   K

3 **Write** اُكْتُبْ

A ___ C ___ E ___ G ___ I ___ K ___

M ___ O ___ Q ___ S ___ U ___ W ___ Y ___

F   L   Z   B   R   N   D   X   V   P   H   T   J

4 **Listen and write** اِسْتَمِعْ واكْتُبْ

Tea?

Yes, please.

No, thank you.

Lesson 14   Review   مُراجَعة

1   Capital letters   ١ الحُروف الكَبيرة

A B C D E F G
H I J K L M N
O P Q R S T U
V W X Y Z

2   Numbers   الأَرْقام

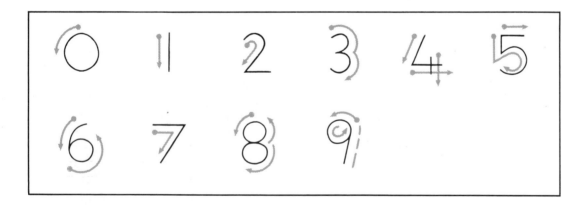

0 1 2 3 4 5
6 7 8 9

3 Say قُلْ

A H J K
B C D E G P T V
F L M N S X Z
I Y
O
Q U W
R

4 What is it? ما هو؟

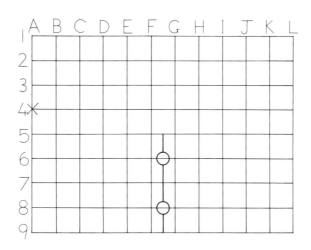

A4, B3, C2, D1, E1, F5, G5, H1, I1, J2,
K3, L4, K5, J4, I3, I9, D9, D3, C4, B5, A4.

5 What is it? ما هي؟

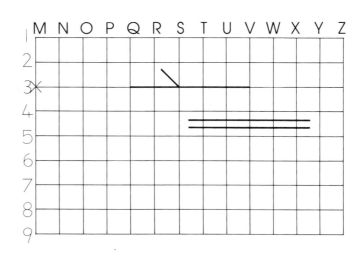

M3, Q3, R1, U1, V3, Y3, Z2, Z3,
Z6, X6, W7, V6, R6, Q7, P6, M6, M3.

Lesson 15

1 A B C   a b c

a a a a a a a a a a a a

b b b b b b b b b b b b b

c c c c c c c c c c c c

2 Match ماثِلْ

a   Abdullah, Bahrain, Salalah

b   Habiba, Abu Dhabi, Aqaba

c   Damascus, welcome, car

31

ab ‌ab

cab ‌cab

Look!	اُنْظُرْ!

A a   Amman,   Anwar,   and

B b   Balbek,   Habbib,   cab

C c   Cairo,   Charles,   welcome

1 D E F d e f

Hello. I'm Ahmed.

My name's **Daoud**.

d   d   d   d   d   d   d   d   d   d   d   d

e   e   e   e   e   e   e   e   e   e   e   e

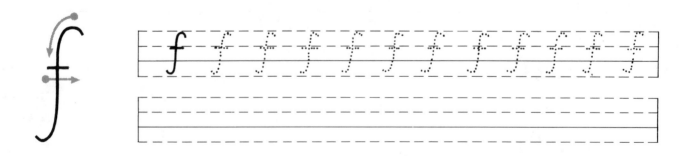

f   f   f   f   f   f   f   f   f   f   f   f

2 Match مائِلْ

d   Saeed, Riyadh, Jordan

e   Waleed, name, hello

f   Lateefa, Taif, from

3 Match مائِلْ

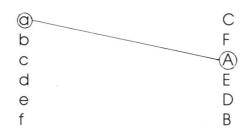

ⓐ   C
b   F
c   Ⓐ
d   E
e   D
f   B

4 Write اُكْتُبْ

bed   bed

bad   bad

face   face

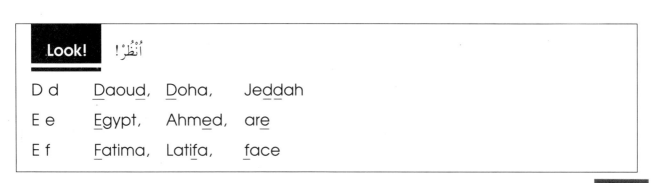

Look!	اُنْظُرْ!

D d   Daoud,   Doha,   Jeddah

E e   Egypt,   Ahmed,   are

E f   Fatima,   Latifa,   face

1 G H I g h i

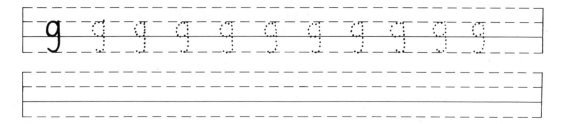

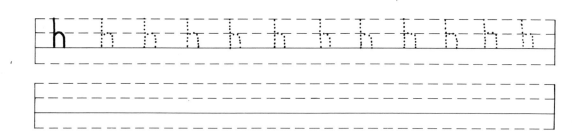

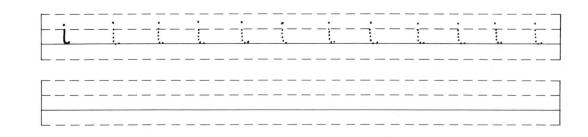

2 Match مائِل

g   George, Algeria, England

h   Salah, Sharjah, thanks

i   Ibrahim, Saudi Arabia, fine

3 Write اُكْتُبْ

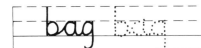
big big

bag bag

head head

4 Write اُكْتُبْ

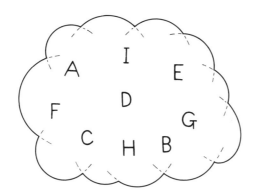

a ___ b ___ c ___ d ___ e ___ f ___ g ___ h ___ i ___

Look!	اُنْظُرْ!

G g   George, garage

H h   Ahmed   Hassan, happy

I i   I'm from Irbid in Jordan.

Lesson 18

1 JKL jkl

2 Match مائِل

j   Haji, Khadija, Sharjah

k   Kirkuk, Sheikh, thanks

l   Latifa, capital letter

3 Write اُكْتُبْ

jack jack

ball ball

Haji Haji

4 Match مَاثِلْ

```
j   b   d   a   j   i   k   b   f   h   c   j   e   j   a   g   i
k   h   k   b   h   j   a   k   l   c   d   k   i   j   e   f   k
l   l   a   c   l   d   b   l   f   a   h   g   e   i   l   k   j
```

Look!	اُنْظُرْ!

J j   Jordan,   Haji,   jeep

K k   Kerak,   Bakker,   jacket

L l   Lulwa,   Algeria,   small letter

Lesson 19   Review مُراجَعة

1   Match ماثِلْ

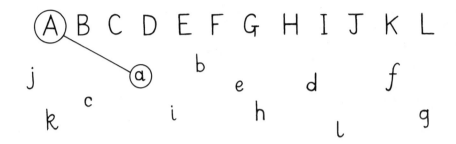

2   Write اُكْتُبْ

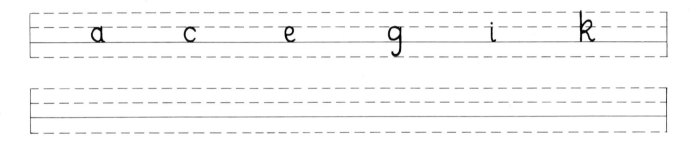

3   Write اُكْتُبْ

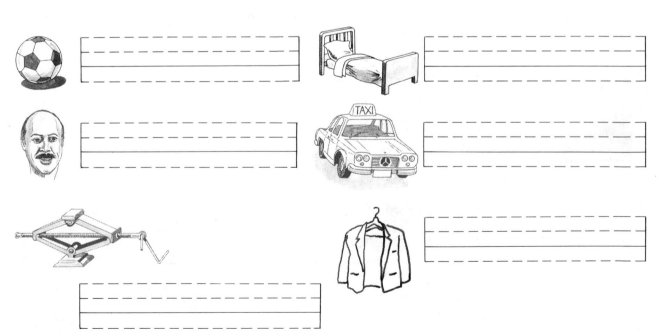

4 Listen and write اِسْتَمِعْ واكْتُبْ

Write small letters.

5 Say قُلْ

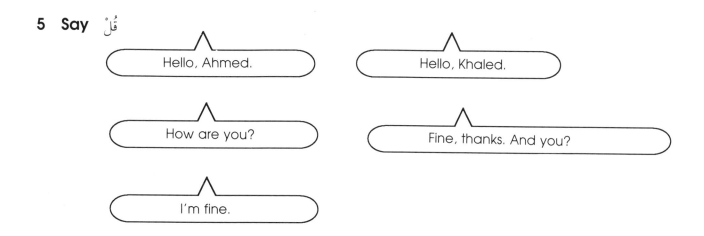

Hello, Ahmed.

Hello, Khaled.

How are you?

Fine, thanks. And you?

I'm fine.

A
Hello, ...
How are you?
I'm fine.

B
Hello, ...
Fine, thanks. And you?

WORDS	كَلِمات

capital letter حَرْف كَبير
small letter حَرْف صَغير

bad	سَيِّئ	bed	سَرير	car	سَيّارة	head	رَأْس
bag	مِحْفظة	big	كَبير	face	وَجْه	jack	رافِعة
ball	كُرَة	cab (taxi)	تَكْسي	goal	هَدَف	jacket	سُتْرة

40

1 M N O   m n o

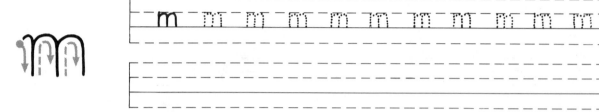

m

n

o

2 Match ماثِل

m   I'm from Dammam. My name's Fatima.

n   My name's Hannan. I'm from Lebanon.

o   Hello, Noor. How are you?

Look!	اُنْظُرْ!	**'m = am**

	I'm fine.	I am fine.
	I'm Ali.	I am Ali.
	I'm from Amman.	I am from Amman.

3 Write اُكْتُبْ

I'm fine   I am fine

man   and

no   not   not bad

book   good

Look!	اُنْظُرْ!

M m   Mo<u>hamm</u>ad, <u>M</u>uscat, <u>m</u>an

N n   <u>N</u>adia, Ha<u>nn</u>an, <u>n</u>ame

O o   <u>O</u>man, <u>O</u>mar, J<u>o</u>rdan, g<u>oo</u>d

1 **P Q R** p q r

Yes.

Can I have your passport, please?

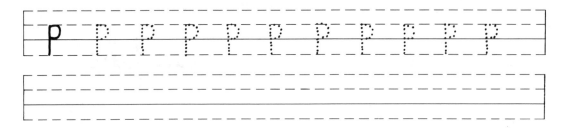

p p p p p p p p p p p p

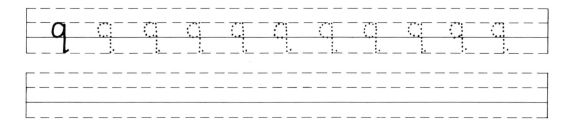

q q q q q q q q q q q q

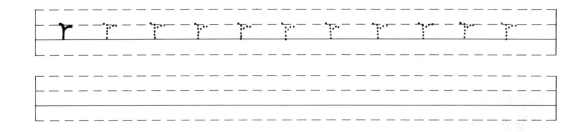

r r r r r r r r r r r r

2 **Match** ماثِل

p   Aleppo, pizza, passport

q   Aqaba, Tariq, queen

r   Morocco, Samira, recorder

3 Write اُكْتُب

pen pen   radio radio

car car   park park

are are   jeep jeep

No parking No parking

4 Write اُكْتُب

a   d e g   j k   n p r

Look!	أُنْظُرْ!
P p	Pepsi, Petra, happy, pick-up, please
R r	Rashid, Jordan, birthday, car
Q q	Qatar, Abdul Qader, Iraq, Tawfiq

Lesson 22

1 STU stu

s

t

u

2 Match ماثِل

s   What's your name? My name's Hassan.

t   United Arab Emirates, Kuwait, football

u   Damascus, Hussain, How are you?

45

<table>
<tr>
<td>

Look! أُنْظُرْ!

's = is

My name's Ali.   My name is Ali.

</td>
</tr>
</table>

3 Write أُكْتُبْ

qu   queen

   mosque   please

th   the   thanks

My name's Tariq

4 Match مائِلْ

A B C D E F G H I J K L M N O P Q R S T U

s p j l a n u e r t i o d c h q m f b g k

<table>
<tr>
<td>

Look! أُنْظُرْ!

S s   Sousse, Sudan, Yes please.

T t   Tunisia, Beirut, what

U u   United Kingdom, Luxor, mosque

</td>
<td></td>
</tr>
</table>

1 V W v w

How are you, Warqa'?

I'm very well, thanks.

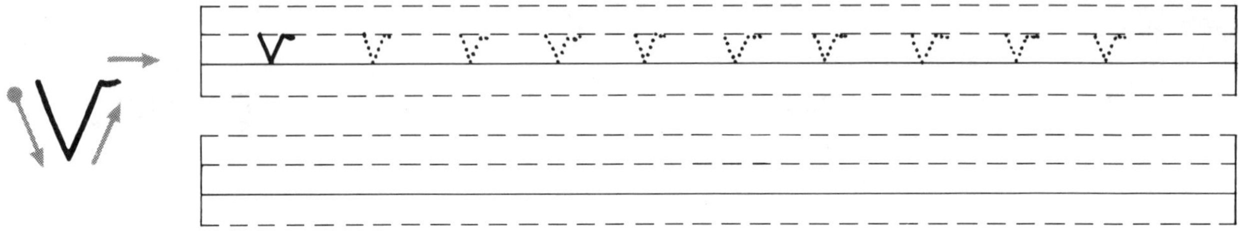

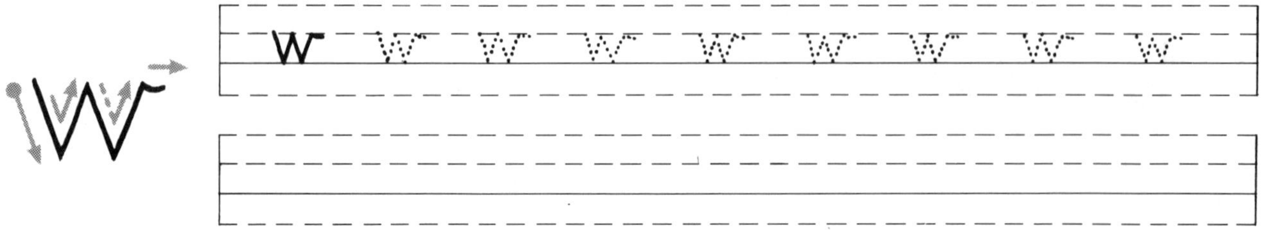

V v v v v v v v v v

W w w w w w w w w w

2 **Match** ماثِل

v Liverpool, television, video recorder, live

w Awad, Kuwait, New York, what, where, how

3 Write اُكْتُب

live   have

very well   woman

what   where

I live in Awali.

Look! اُنْظُرْ!   V v   I live in Vienna.

W w   Waleed is from Aswan. Where are you from?

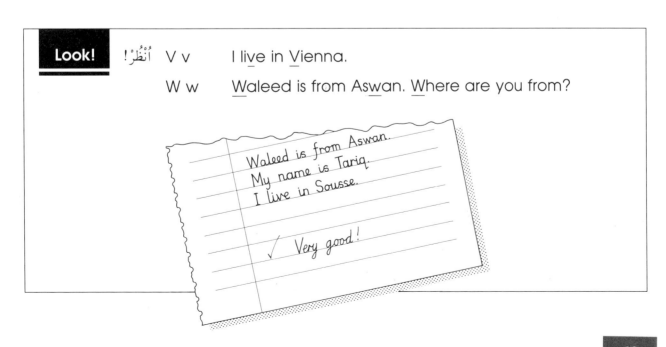

Waleed is from Aswan.
My name is Tariq.
I live in Sousse.

✓ Very good!

Lesson 24

1   X Y Z x y z

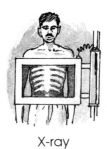

X-ray

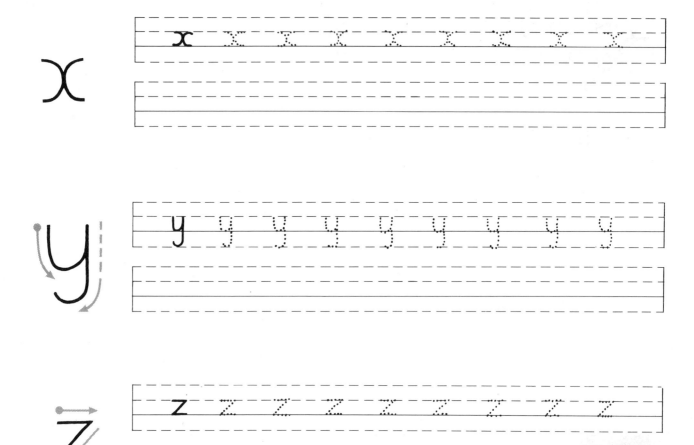

2   Match مائِل

x   Sfax, Alexandria, Luxor, express

y   Libya, Syria, thank you

z   Gaza, Azraq, Fez, Hejaz

box   Luxor

yes   you   your

my   lazy

Aziza is very lazy.

Look!	اُنْظُرْ!

X x   I'm from Alexandria in Egypt.

Y y   My name's Yacoob. Are you from Yemen?

Z z   Aziz and Zuhair live in Zarqa' in Jordan.

Lesson 25   **Review** مُراجَعة

1   Small letters الحُروف الصَّغيرة

a b c d e f g h i j

k l m n o p q r

s t u v w x y z

2   Match ماثِلْ

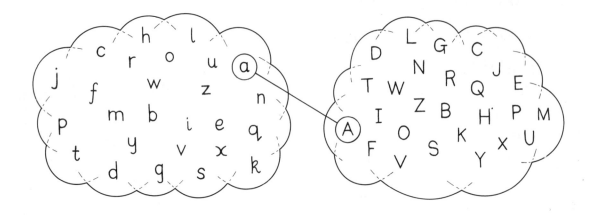

3 Write اُكْتُب

a   c   e   g   i   k   m

o   q   s   u   w   y

4 Write اُكْتُب

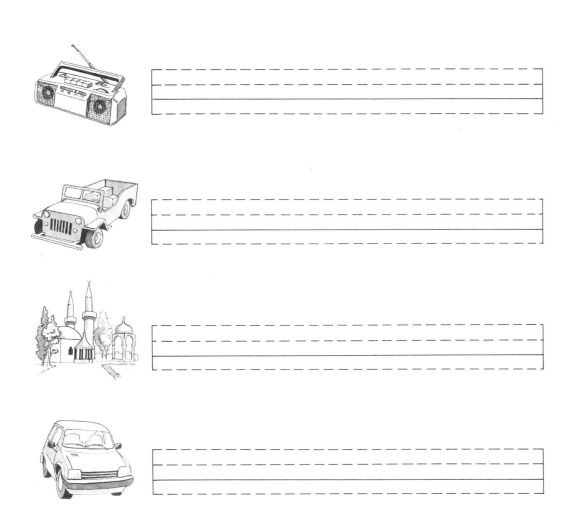

5 Listen and write اِسْتَمِعْ واكْتُبْ

WORDS كَلِمات

book	كِتاب
box	صُندوق
car	سَيّارة
fine	جَيِّد
good	جَيِّد
jeep	سَيّارة جيب
lazy	كَسول
mosque	مَسْجِد
no	لا
park	حَديقة
pen	قَلَم
please	مِن فَضْلِكَ
queen	مَلِكة
radio	راديو
thanks	شُكْرًا
the	أل
very	جِدًّا
very well	جَيِّد جِدًّا
what	ماذا
where	أَيْنَ
woman	اِمْرَأة
yes	نَعَم

1   Names

A   Ahmed
B   Badria
C   Charles
D   Daoud
E   Essa
F   Fatima
G   Ghazi
H   Hannan
I   Ibrahim
J   Jameela
K   Khadijah
L   Latifa
M   Mona

N   Nadia
O   Omar
P   Paul
Q   Qassim
R   Rashid
S   Samira
T   Tawfiq
U   Usame
V   Victoria
W   Warqa'
X   _____
Y   Yacoub
Z   Zeinab

Write   ‫اُكْتُب‬

Ahmed

Badria

(lined writing spaces)

2 Read اِقْرَأْ

Hello, Mary. How are you?

I'm fine thanks. How are you?

Very well thanks.

What's your name, please?

My name's Ahmed Yacoub.

Can I have your passport, please?

3 Say قُلْ

Ask three students   اِسْأَلْ ثَلاثَةَ تَلامِيذ

A

What's your name, please?

B

My name's . . .

1   Name: _____   _____

2   Name: _____   _____

3   Name: _____   _____

How are you ?

How are you ?

I'm very well, thanks.

What's your name ?

My name's Ahmed Yacoub.

Can I have your passport, please ?

Lesson 27   Where are you from?

مِنْ أَيْنَ أَنْتَ؟

1   Match the city with the country.   مَاثِلْ بَيْنَ المَدينة والبَلَد

Egypt, Qatar, Syria, Bahrain, Iraq, Oman, Kuwait, United Arab Emirates, Lebanon.

	City	Country
1	Cairo	Egypt
2	Beirut	
3	Dubai	
4	Riyadh	
5	Damascus	
6	Amman	
7	Manama	
8	Baghdad	
9	Fehaheel	

2   Read   اِقْرَأْ

3 Say قُلْ

Ask three students   إِسْأَلْ ثَلاثَةَ تَلاميذ

A	B
Where are you from?	**I'm from . . .**
Where's that?	**It's in . . . .**

	Name	From
1	Samira	Aswan, Egypt
2		
3		

4 Write اُكْتُبْ

Where are you from?

Where are you from?

I'm from Gabes.

Where's that?

It's in Tunisia.

5   Write أُكْتُب

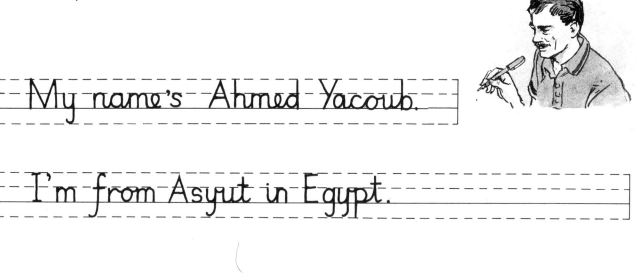

My name's Ahmed Yacoub.

I'm from Asyut in Egypt.

What's your name? Where are you from?

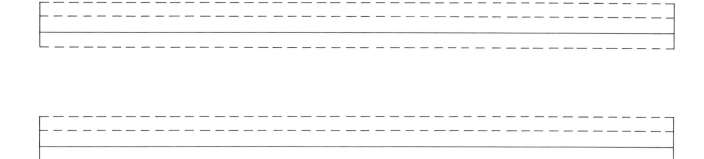

60

Lesson 28　Numbers　الأَرْقام

1　Numbers　0–10

0	zero (oh)
1	one
2	two
3	three
4	four
5	five
6	six
7	seven
8	eight
9	nine
10	ten

2　Write　اُكْتُب

zero zero

one one

two two

three three

61

four four

five five

six six

seven seven

eight eight

nine nine

ten ten

3 Read اِقْرَأْ

What's the time, please?

It's nine o'clock.

4 Write اُكْتُبْ

What's the time? كَم السّاعَةُ؟

It's 3 o'clock

5 Say قُلْ

What's the time, please?
It's . . . o'clock.

Lesson 29   Punctuation   عَلامات التَّرْقيم

1   Look   اُنْظُرْ

exclamation mark   عَلامَة التَّعَجُّب

Hello!

's = is   question mark   عَلامة الاسْتِفْهام

What's your name?   ما اسْمُكَ؟

full stop

My name's Samira.   إِسْمي سَميرة. نُقْطة

'm = am   comma   فاصِلة

I'm very well, thank you.   إنَّني بِخَيْر، والحَمْد لله

.   =   full stop   نُقْطة
,   =   comma   فاصِلة
?   =   question mark   عَلامة تَعَجُّب
!   =   exclamation mark   عَلامة اسْتِفْهام

2   Write: .   ,   ?   '   !   اُكْتُبْ

My name's Hussain

I m from Abu Dhabi

Where are you from

Are you from Jeddah

Welcome

Can I have tea please

What s the time

It s six o clock

3 Capital letters الحُروف الكَبيرة

We use capital letters at the beginning of – نَسْتَعْمِلُ الحروف الكَبيرة في أَوَّلِ

names الأَسْماء

Ahmed, Fatima, Lulwa, Waleed.

cities المُدُن

Beirut, Muscat, Abu Dhabi

countries البُلْدان

Jordan, Yemen, England

We use capital letters at the beginning of a sentence.

نَسْتَعْمِل الحُروف الكَبيرة في بِدايَة الجُملة

Where are you from?
My name's Khalifa.
It's seven o'clock.
How are you?

We also write capital I – when it is alone. وأَيْضًا نَكْتب الحَرْف I كَبيراً عندما يَكون وَحْدَه

I am from Bahrain.

4 Write اُكْتُبْ

Put in the capital letters. ضَع الحُروفَ الكَبيرة

a my name's badria yousef.

b i'm from fehaheel in kuwait.

c what's the time?

d are you from england?

1 Find 11 countries جِدْ ١١ بَلَدًا

```
X A L G E R I A B Y K U
D F E O Z V K J T M Q X
S L B K W S Q O L F Y B
Y S A U D I A R A B I A
R B N W J K Z D F L R A
I P O A B O M A N X A T
A C N I W Y P N R N Q X
O Y D T Z F J B E R Q O
O E U N I T E D A R A B
E M I R A T E S X B T C
Z E G Y P T D R W Q A S
V N H B A H R A I N R O
```

2 Write اُكْتُبْ

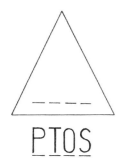

a   PTOS

b   ON KSIGMNO

c   ECWOMEL   _____ TO SAUDI ARABIA

d   ON KAPIGRN

3 Numbers الأَرْقام

a reeht   _three_

b net   _____

c xsi   _____

d vense   _____

e enni   _____

f noe   _____

g urfo   _____

h wot   _____

i veif   _____

j heitg   _____

4 What is it? ما هي؟

a

b

c

d

e

f

g

h

1	park
2	box
3	mosque
4	ball
5	book
6	passport
7	car
8	man

69

5 Match the words مائِلْ بَيْنَ الكَلِمات

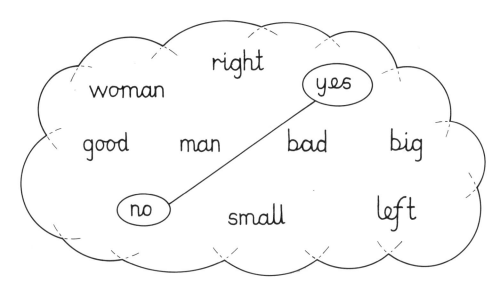

6 Cities مُدُن

Find 10 cities جِدْ ١٠ مُدُن

a   R ___ Y ___ ___ H

b   D ___ ___ A I

c   ___ ___ S C ___ T

d   B ___ ___ R U ___

e   C ___ ___ R O

f   A ___ M A ___

g   D ___ M ___ S ___ ___ S

h   J ___ ___ ___ A H

i   B ___ G H ___ ___ D

j   M ___ N ___ M ___

Appendix

Numbers and letters

Numbers

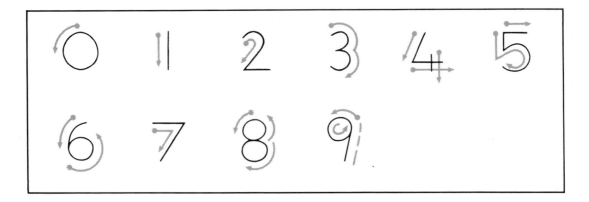

0	1	2	3	4	5	6	7	8	9	10
zero	one	two	three	four	five	six	seven	eight	nine	ten
٠	١	٢	٣	٤	٥	٦	٧	٨	٩	١٠

Capital letters

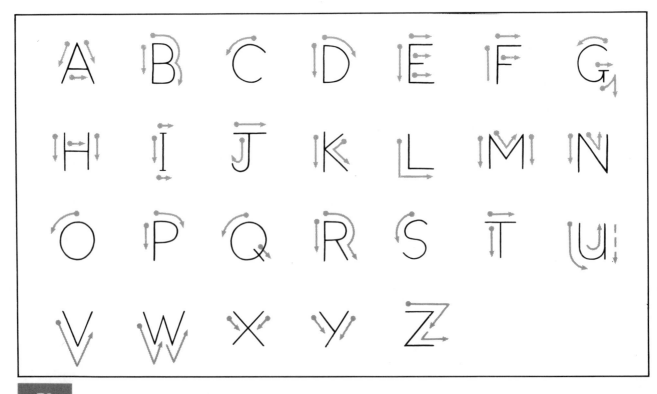

Small letters

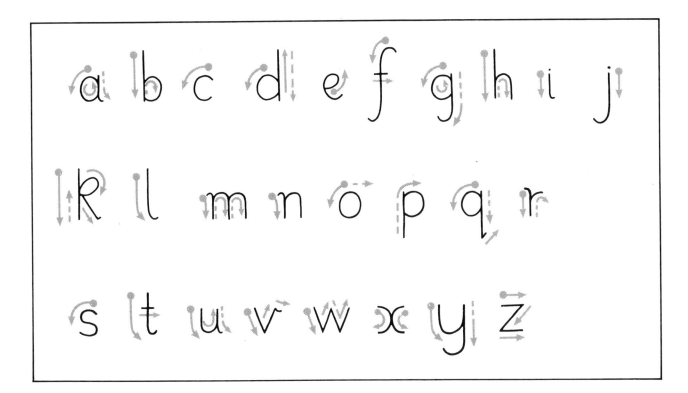

A B C D E F G H I J K L M N O P Q R S T U V W X Y Z

a b c d e f g h i j k l m n o p q r s t u v w x y z

a b c d e f g h i j k l m n o p q r s t u v w x y z

Word list قائِمة كَلِمات

bad سَيِّئ
bag مِحْفَظة
ball كُرَة
bed سَرير
big كَبير
book كِتاب
box صُنْدوق
cab (taxi) تَكْسي
capital عاصِمة
car سَيّارة
city مَدينة
country بَلَد
express القِطارِ السَّريع
face وَجْه
goal هَدَف
good جَيِّد
head رَأْس
help مُساعَدة
jack رافِعَة
jacket سُتْرَة
jeep سَيّارَة جيب
lazy كَسول
left يَسار
letter حَرْف
live حَيّ
man رَجُل
mosque مَسجِد
number رَقْم
park حَديقة
passport جَواز
pen قَلَم
pick-up شاحِنة
queen مَلِكة
radio راديو
right مُسَجِّلة
small صَغير
television تلفزيون
video recorder مُسجِّلة فيديو
woman اِمْرأَة
x-ray أشِعَّة إكس

Hello. مَرْحَبًا
How are you? كَيْفَ حالُكَ؟
Fine, thanks. بخَيْر والحَمْد لله
I'm fine, thank you. إنَّني بخَيْر والحَمْد لله
I'm very well, thank you. إنَّني بخَيْر والحَمْد لله
Not bad. لا بَأْس

What's your name? ما اسْمُكِ؟
My name's (Badria). إسْمي بَدْرِيَّة
I'm (Badria). أنا بَدْرِيَّة

Welcome to (Egypt). أهْلًا بكَ في مِصْر
Where are you from? مِنْ أَيْنَ أَنْتَ؟
I'm from (Egypt). أنا مِن مِصْر

What's the time? كَم الساعَةُ؟
It's seven o'clock. إنَّها السابِعة

Can I have (your passport), please?

أعْطِني جَوازَكَ مِن فَضْلِكَ

Yes/No. نَعَمْ/ لا

Yes, please. أَجَلْ لو سَمَحْتَ
No, thank you. كَلّا شُكْرًا
Very good. جَيِّدٌ جِدًّا

Stop! Go! قِفْ! سِرْ!

No smoking. التَّدخين مَمْنوع
No parking. الوُقوف مَمْنوع

73